History of America

AMERICA'S
FIRST SETTLEMENTS

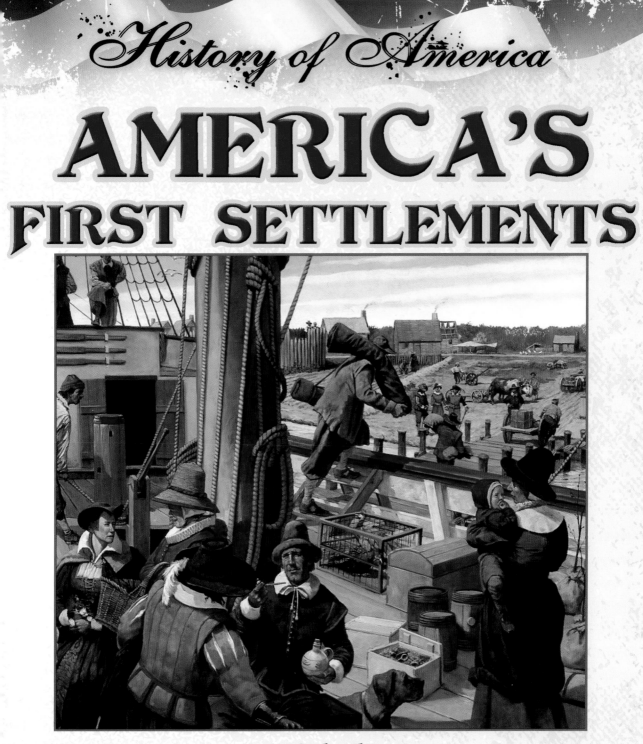

Written by **Linda Thompson**

Educational Media

rourkeeducationalmedia.com

www.rourkeeducationalmedia.com

PHOTO CREDITS:
Courtesy CA Department of Conservation, CA Geological Survey: page 9; Courtesy Historical Society of Pennsylvania: page 28; Courtesy Library of Congress Prints and Photographs Division: pages 5, 6, 7, 8, 9, 10, 13, 14, 15, 16, 17, 18, 19, 20, 21, 22, 24, 25, 26, 30, 32, 33, 34, 35, 37, 39; Courtesy NASA: page 28; Courtesy National Archives and Records Administration: page 40; Courtesy National Oceanic and Atmospheric Administration: page11; Courtesy National Parks Service: pages 23, 43; Courtesy Rohm Padilla: pages 4, 29, 38; Courtesy Charles Reasoner: pages 12, 27; Courtesy U.S. Fish and Wildlife Service: Title Page, page 14.

Edited by Jill Sherman

Cover design by Nicola Stratford, bdpublishing.com

Interior layout by Tara Raymo

Library of Congress PCN Data

Thompson, Linda
  America's First Settlements / Linda Thompson.
  ISBN 978-1-62169-834-0 (hard cover)
  ISBN 978-1-62169-729-9 (soft cover)
  ISBN 978-1-62169-938-5 (e-Book)
Library of Congress Control Number: 2013936382

Also Available as:

Rourke Educational Media
Printed in the United States of America,
North Mankato, Minnesota

rourkeeducationalmedia.com

customerservice@rourkeeducationalmedia.com • PO Box 643328 Vero Beach, Florida 32964

Table of Contents

Chapter 1
Welcome to the New World

Only 20 years after it became independent, the United States doubled in size, thanks to President Thomas Jefferson's wise purchase of the Louisiana Territory from France. Within 50 years, the country stretched across immense plains and towering mountain ranges to touch the Pacific Ocean.

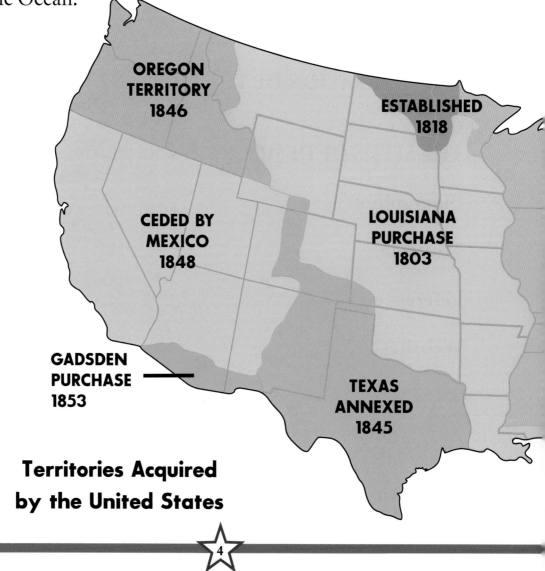

OREGON TERRITORY 1846

ESTABLISHED 1818

CEDED BY MEXICO 1848

LOUISIANA PURCHASE 1803

GADSDEN PURCHASE 1853

TEXAS ANNEXED 1845

Territories Acquired by the United States

How the United States grew so fast in such a short time is an amazing tale. But the expansion that took place after the American Revolution was only a logical continuation of the westbound movement Europeans had begun in 1492 with Christopher Columbus. Before that date America had a few visitors, but they did not bring permanent settlers. The voyages of Columbus were a milestone in American history because they eventually brought great **hordes** of people from across the sea. And once religious and political leaders decided a region might be worthy of settlement, families began to arrive.

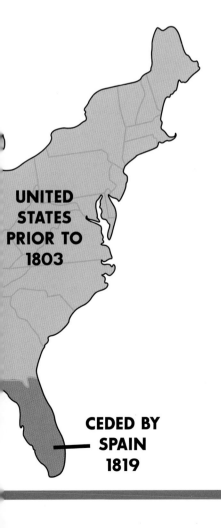

UNITED STATES PRIOR TO 1803

CEDED BY SPAIN 1819

Christopher Columbus (1451-1506)

THE VIKINGS

More than 500 years before Columbus, Norse, or Scandinavian, seamen known as **Vikings** had sailed to the coast of North America.

Leif Eriksson spies the New World.

One of them, Leif Eriksson, landed in 1000 on the coast of what was probably Newfoundland and called it Vinland. His followers tried to live there, but constant battles with Native Americans made them give up after a few years.

However, the first European explorers of the New World were not looking for new places for people to live. The sailors who arrived from Spain, France, England, Portugal, and other countries were actually seeking a sea route to the Orient. India, China, Indonesia, the Spice Islands, and their neighbors produced highly desirable goods such as silks, jewelry, and spices. The Italian adventurer, Marco Polo, had helped introduce these lands and their products to Europe in the 13th century. But the routes Marco Polo pioneered, leading eastward, were often blocked by hostile forces or controlled by groups that demanded high taxes.

For the first time, Europeans were building ships that were large and seaworthy enough to sail into the uncharted waters to the west. Christopher Columbus, an Italian whose voyage was paid for by Spain, was one of the first explorers to try to reach the Orient by sailing west. In 1492, he landed on an island in the Bahamas. Thinking it was India, he called the **indigenous people** he encountered "Indians." Columbus made several more voyages, the last in 1502 to 1503, visiting present-day **Hispaniola**, Cuba, which he thought was Japan, and Jamaica. He died in Spain in 1506, still believing he had reached the Far East.

After ten long weeks at sea, Christopher Columbus lands in America in 1492.

One of Columbus's goals had been to find precious metal. The queen of Spain had promised him 10 percent of all he could bring back. Some of the native people he met wore tiny gold ornaments in their ears. In the rivers of Hispaniola, the sailors saw small amounts of gold. When Columbus returned to Spain, he exaggerated, writing that he had seen "many wide rivers of which the majority contain gold." On his next voyage, finding no gold, he took many Native American slaves instead. Some were sent by ship to Spain but they did not survive the voyage.

Columbus's voyage was met with friendly indigenous people bearing gifts for the newcomers.

A gold nugget.

The Spaniards forced hundreds of natives to work in Hispaniola agricultural fields or in the mines, which yielded a little gold after a great deal of digging. The Spaniards were harsh masters, and within two years the native population had been reduced by half, down from about 250,000.

PONCE DE LEON SPOTS U.S. MAINLAND

The first European to sight the mainland of the North American continent was Spanish explorer **Juan Ponce de León** on March 27, 1513. He named the land *La Florida*, or *Land of Flowers* in Spanish. For the next 50 years, Spain tried unsuccessfully to establish a colony in Florida.

Juan Ponce de León (1474-1521)

This pattern would be repeated again and again over the next 50 years, during which Spain conquered Mexico, Peru, and Central America, and Portugal claimed Brazil. The invaders' main goal was to find gold, and their second goal was to convert the indigenous people to Christianity. Unfortunately, every landing of the Europeans had severely harmful effects on the millions of native people who already lived there.

ST. AUGUSTINE

The oldest permanent European settlement in the United States is St. Augustine, Florida, founded in 1565. The Spanish king, Felipe II, sent Admiral Pedro Menendez de Aviles to build a fort on Florida's shores and keep France out. Menendez destroyed a French garrison on the St. Johns River. He then built a town that for nearly 200 years was home to Spaniards, Native Americans, Africans, and mixed-blood residents. In 1763, Spain traded Florida to England for Cuba, and St. Augustine became an English colony.

Ruins of the fort at St. Augustine, Florida.

A Spanish explorer proclaims to Native Americans that they are now subjects of the king and must become Christians.

In the early 16th century, Spain, Portugal, England, France, and the Netherlands had major naval forces. Competition to colonize the New World and harvest its treasures increased rapidly. In 1588, the English brought Spain's domination of the Atlantic Ocean to a standstill by defeating Spain's great armada, or fleet of warships. From then on, ships from other countries could come and go more freely and settlement of America began **in earnest**. Colonial territories with names such as New England, New Amsterdam, and New France began to crop up across the New World.

Ships of the Spanish Armada.

Cabot was the first person to set foot on Canada (or Maine) for the English. He gave people the knowledge to look at the globe in a different way, and found new ways to travel around the world.

JOHN CABOT CLAIMS CANADA FOR ENGLAND

In 1497 an Italian explorer, Giovanni Caboto, sailed along the eastern shores of Canada. Known to the English as John Cabot, he was seeking a trade route to the Orient for Henry VII of England. The following year, Cabot explored the Atlantic coast from Baffin Island, Canada, to Maryland. These voyages gave England a claim to the northeast coast of North America.

Chapter 2
New France and New Netherland

River otters were one of the primary sources of furs.

The realization that Columbus had not reached the Orient was not as disappointing to the seafaring nations as it might have been, for two reasons. First, rumors were spreading about rich cargoes of gold and silver that Spanish treasure ships were now bringing back from the **West Indies.** Secondly, explorers reported that fishing in the waters off North America was excellent!

Jacques Cartier's fleet sailing on the St. Lawrence River in Canada.

Sixteenth-century adventurers searched for a great river through North America that would serve as a short cut to the Far East. In 1524, France sent a navigator from Italy, Giovanni da Verrazano, to explore the coastline from Newfoundland in Canada to North Carolina. He did not find passage to the East, but his exploration gave France a claim to that area. Ten years later, Jacques Cartier sailed up the St. Lawrence River reaching the areas of Quebec and Montreal. France began harvesting the area's fish and animal skins. It did not try to establish colonies but sent annual fishing fleets to the waters off Canada. By the early 1600s, France had also developed a very profitable fur trade.

In 1534 Jacques Cartier was warmly welcomed by the resident Iroquois and learned that two rivers led farther west to lands where gold, silver, copper, and spices abounded.

Samuel de Champlain (1574-1635)

In 1608 French navigator Samuel de Champlain founded a trading post at Quebec, the first permanent European settlement in Canada. Only 9 of the original 32 colonists survived the winter, but more settlers arrived the following summer. Champlain explored much of the eastern coast as far south as Cape Cod. In 1613 and 1615, he sailed up the St. Lawrence River, eventually reaching Lake Huron and Lake Ontario.

Champlain, who is considered the father of New France, discouraged farmers from settling but welcomed Catholic missionaries to help convert Native American allies to Christianity. Within a few decades, a dozen missions could be found in the backwoods of New France.

By the end of the 17th century, René-Robert Cavelier, had claimed the entire Mississippi River watershed and the future site of New Orleans, Louisiana, for France. But New France's emphasis on hunting and fishing, instead of farming and making trade goods, meant that France would never be able to use the great river for commercial shipping. Its scant population would also never be able to defend it when necessary.

New York City, which today leads American cities in population, was originally a Dutch settlement. In 1610 English navigator **Henry Hudson**, working for the Dutch East India Company, sailed into the mouth of what would later be called the Hudson River. He traveled as far north as present-day Albany, New York, and claimed the entire Hudson River valley for the Dutch. In 1614 the New Netherlands Company of Amsterdam built the first Dutch settlement on an island in the Hudson River. The settlement was called Fort Nassau. It was abandoned in 1617 because of frequent floods. A few years later, Fort Orange, now Albany, was built on the west side of the river. Like the French, the Dutch focused heavily on fur trading and less on farming.

In 1609 Henry Hudson's ships entered the harbor and explored a stretch of the river that now bears his name.

THE DUTCH TRADE IN SLAVES

The Dutch brought the first slave ship to the North American continent when it landed at Jamestown in 1619. At first Africans were listed as servants, but they were bought, sold, and treated as slaves. From 1500 to 1800, 12 million African slaves came to the New World, but only about a half million were shipped to the North American colonies. About six million were sent to Central and South America and about five million to the West Indies.

Captives in an African village being sent into slavery after coming to the New World.

The East India Company had successfully traded with Indonesia and other Far East countries. In 1621 the Netherlands formed the West India Company to conduct business in Africa and North America. It sent 30 Dutch families to Hudson Bay in 1626, and they settled on what is now Manhattan

Dutch men offering a trade to Native Americans.

Island. This village, Fort Amsterdam, would become the capital of the Dutch colony. By 1630, about 300 people lived there.

In 1626 a director of the West India Company, Peter Minuit, arrived to administer the struggling colony. In one of the most amazing bargains of history, he traded 60 guilders worth of cloth, kettles, hatchets, and other goods to a group of Delaware Native Americans for the island of Manhattan. This was nearly 34 square miles (88 square kilometers) of valuable land. Although the U.S. dollar had not yet been created, the price is often said to have equaled about 24 dollars. The Native Americans who sold Manhattan lived elsewhere, and since they had no concept of buying or selling land they may have thought they were merely selling hunting rights. In any case, the Dutch took ownership of Manhattan and named it New Amsterdam.

WALL STREET

Peter Stuyvesant tried to ward off the English invasion of New Amsterdam in 1653. The city was at the southern tip of the island, and the Dutch decided to build a wall across the north end of the settlement. Made of 12-foot-high (3.6-meter) logs, it stretched for half a mile across the island. No English attack came that year, but the wall remained and a street near it was named Wall Street. In 1729, the first stock exchange office opened at 22 Wall Street and the name took on a meaning that remains world famous today.

Wall Street in New York in 1847.

As settlements grew, the Dutch colonists carried out harsh campaigns against Native Americans. Also, the Dutch created ill will by taking over Fort Cristina, a Swedish colony of about 500 people that had begun

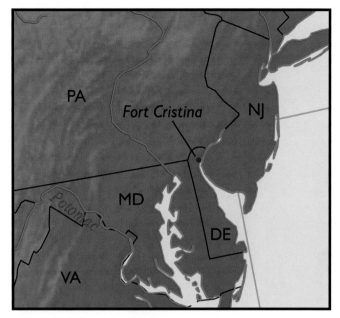

Fort Cristina is near present-day Wilmington, Delaware.

in 1638. The Dutch director, Peter Stuyvesant considered New Sweden a threat to commerce and **annexed** the colony in 1655. But in less than 10 years, the tables had turned. In 1664 Stuyvesant was forced to surrender New Netherland with its 9,000 colonists to the English.

England had many reasons to declare war on Holland, including colonial interests and competition for African slaves and ivory. Both countries were eager to dominate the seas, along with the wealth now flowing to Europe from faraway lands. So Charles II, king of England, decided to give a gift, New Netherland, to his 30-year-old brother, James Stuart, Duke of York. All King Charles had to do was go get it.

Penn wanted the land to be a place where people of different languages and customs could live together.

Charles II sent four **frigates** to New Amsterdam, and since he had no navy to defend the colony, Stuyvesant surrendered without a fight. Charles gave his brother the land that now makes up New York State as well as parts of Maine, Connecticut, Pennsylvania, New Jersey, and Delaware. The English renamed New Amsterdam New York, and gave the entire province the same name. The Duke gave New Jersey to two of his friends. Then he gave another young settler, William Penn, a large piece of land that later became Pennsylvania.

Chapter 3

Jamestown and Roanoke

English writers and promoters tried to lure people to America in the early 1600s. For example, a poem about Virginia titled *Ode to the Virginian Voyage* by Michael Drayton was widely published.

> *Virginia, Earth's only paradise.*
> *Where Nature hath in store Fowle, Venison and Fish,*
> *And the Fruitfull'st Soyle, without your Toyle,*
> *Three harvests more, all greater than your Wish,*
> *And the ambitious Vine, crownes with his purple Masse,*
> *The cedar reaching hie to kisse the Sky,*
> *The Cypresse, Pine and use-full Sassafras.*

You brave heroic minds,
Worthy your country's name,
That honour still pursue,
Go and subdue!
Whilst loit'ring hinds
Lurk here at home with shame.
Britons, you stay too long;
Quickly aboard bestow you,
And with a merry gale
Swell your stretch'd sail,
With vows as strong
As the winds that blow you!

Your course securely steer,
West and by south forth keep;
Rocks, lee-shores, nor shoals,
When AEolus scowls,
You need not fear,
So absolute the deep.

And cheerfully at sea
Success you still entice
To get the pearl and gold,
And ours to hold
Virginia,
Earth's only paradise!

Where nature hath in store
Fowl, venison, and fish,
And the fruitful'st soil,
Without your toil,
Three harvests more,
All greater than your wish.

And the ambitious vine
Crowns with his purple mass,
The cedar reaching high
To kiss the sky,
The cypress, pine,
And useful sassafras;

To whose the golden age
Still nature's laws doth give;
No other cares that tend
But them to defend
From winter's age,
That long there doth not live.

When as the luscious smell
Of that delicious land,
Above the seas that flows,
The clear wind throws,
Your hearts to swell
Approaching the dear strand.

In kenning of the shore,
Thanks to God first given,
O you, the happiest men,
Be frolic then!
Let cannons roar
Frighting the wide heaven.

And in regions far
Such heroes bring ye forth,
As those from whom we came;
And plant our name
Under that star
Not known unto our north.

And, as there plenty grows
Of laurel everywhere,
Apollo's sacred tree,
You may it see
A poet's brows
To crown, that may sing there.

Thy voyages attend,
Industrious Hakluyt,
Whose reading shall enflame
Men to seek fame,
And much commend
To after-times thy wit.

English settlers bound for America.

Of course, the reality of the New World, a treacherous sea crossing, difficult weather, harsh soil conditions, and indigenous people who resisted foreigners, did not exactly add up to a paradise. Most people who left London were sailors, single, adventurers, farmers, the unemployed, and some **convicts**.

WHY DID ENGLAND ENCOURAGE EMIGRATION?

England was overpopulated in the 1600s, with limited opportunities for all but the upper class. One solution was to persuade poorer folks to sail for America. Merchants hoped to sell woolen goods in parts of North America where the climate was cold and to grow olive trees and grapes where the climate was warm. England had a religious interest as well. It wanted to limit the influence of Catholic countries such as Spain and France in the New World. Finally, England hoped that large amounts of gold and silver similar to those found in Peru and Mexico might exist in North America.

The first attempt at an English colony in the New World happened even before 1600. In 1585 Sir Walter Raleigh sent about a hundred men to Roanoke Island in Virginia, off the coast of what is now North Carolina. Virginia was a poorly

Sir Walter Raleigh (1552-1618)

defined land, larger than it is today. Raleigh and others had named it in honor of England's Virgin Queen, Elizabeth I. A year later Sir Francis Drake, a sea dog returning from a raid on Spanish ships in the West Indies, stopped at Roanoke. He found the remaining colonists ready to give up. Many had been killed by Native Americans or died of hunger or diseases such as malaria and dysentery. Drake took the survivors back to England. Another ship left 15 men at the colony to defend it.

But Raleigh was determined and sent another 120 settlers, including 17 women, to Roanoke in three ships in 1587. Captain John White led the new colony. His daughter, Elenora, and her husband had come to Roanoke with him. Within a few months, they had a child and named her Virginia Dare. She was the first English child born in America.

Unfortunately, England was at war with Spain and needed all of its resources to defeat the Spanish armada. England neglected the colony until 1590. When more ships arrived at Roanoke, not a single person could be found. Only some armor, maps, rusting iron, and the ruins of structures

Sir Francis Drake (1540-1596)

SEA DOGS

In the mid-16th century, a number of sea dogs, men who combined fighting with sailing, adventure, and trade became famous in England. Among them were Francis Drake and Walter Raleigh. Many of the sea dogs were knighted by the queen of England, earning the title "Sir."

remained, along with the word "Croatoan" carved on a tree. The sailors guessed that any survivors had headed toward Croatoan Island, 100 miles (160 kilometers) south of the Carolinas. Their fate remains a mystery. Sir Walter Raleigh was said to have lost 40,000 English pounds, about $4 million in today's money, on the ill-fated settlement of Roanoke.

Elenora (1563-1599) and Virginia Dare (1587- year of death unknown)

Remnants of a church tower from the Jamestown settlement is visited today in historic Jamestown.

Sixteen years passed before England was ready to try again. On December 20, 1606, three small ships, named *Susan Constant*, *Godspeed*, and *Discovery*, sailed from London. People were crowded onto these ships sponsored by the Virginia Company of London. After four rough months at sea, they came to Chesapeake Bay, on the Atlantic coast of present-day Virginia. The ships sailed about 60 miles (97 kilometers) up a river that flowed into Chesapeake Bay. The voyagers named it James River after King James I of England.

They pitched tents and called their settlement Jamestown. It became the first permanent English settlement in the New World.

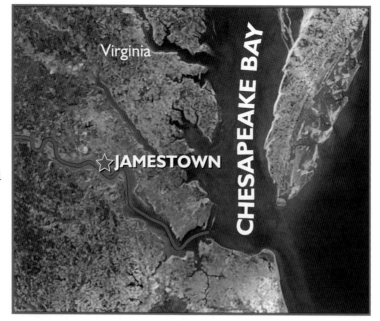

Chesapeake Bay, with the James River indicated in red.

Just like the Roanoke pioneers, the colonists of Jamestown experienced major difficulties. Of the 144 people who sailed from England, only 105 survived the trip. They **disembarked** on May 14, 1607, and 12 days later faced their first battle with Native Americans. They made the mistake of building their forts, church, and homes in a low, swampy area. Many

John Smith (1580-1631)

became ill. In addition to disease, they contended with hunger and exhausting work. Captain John Smith, the colony's first leader, was strict about everybody doing their share. He said, "He that will not work, neither will he eat." After less than two years, only 60 colonists were still alive.

COLONIZATION AS AN INVESTMENT

Like other countries, England lacked the resources to establish and maintain colonies. The royalty granted private companies **charters** to form settlements, first in Virginia and later in New England. The investors' main interest was in trading furs and skins. Investors paid the costs of establishing a colony by buying stock in the company at 12 pounds (about $62 in gold) per share.

The survivors were about to abandon Jamestown when a new ship arrived carrying several hundred men and a new leader, Lord de la Warr. Both he and his successor, Sir Thomas Dale, imposed strict military discipline. The colonists had no hope of owning land because they were working for the benefit of London stockholders. In 1612 their only cash crop was cedar wood. The colony's destiny began to change in 1613 with the introduction of a new crop, tobacco.

In 1616, Pocahontas and her husband, Jamestown colonist John Rolfe, visited England as part of a Virginia Company effort to raise funds to enlarge its colonies in North America.

The introduction of tobacco to Jamestown can be credited to one Jamestown colonist, John Rolfe. Rolfe is also famous for marrying a young Powhatan woman named Pocahontas. Rolfe brought seeds of a mild strain of tobacco from the West Indies, and crossed them with native tobacco seeds, creating a new variety. Virginia tobacco became instantly popular with English traders, storekeepers, and consumers. By 1618, Virginia was exporting 50,000 pounds (22,700 kilograms) of tobacco a year to England. Although King James stated that tobacco was unhealthy, he did not prohibit its import. The Virginia Company convinced the English **Parliament** that only tobacco could save Jamestown from disaster.

Jamestown's success was also helped by a legal change that allowed colonists to acquire land. After working for seven years, a man could become a tenant farmer. After another 10 years or so, the land he worked became his own. Hundreds of field laborers took advantage of this opportunity and became plantation owners. More women began to join the colony as well. The Virginia Company would send an unmarried woman to any planter who wanted a wife in return for 150 pounds (68 kilograms) of prime tobacco. The creation of families gave the settlers more reason to stay.

Chapter 4
The Separation of the Puritans

During the 16th century England began having religious conflicts as part of a movement throughout the Christian world called the **Reformation**. Some people criticized official church doctrine and wanted to separate completely

from it. They called themselves Puritans because they wanted a pure, or direct link between each individual and God without rituals, saints, popes, and other **intermediaries**.

The Puritans first concern in life was to do God's will and so to receive future happiness.

In 1608 some English Puritans fled to Leyden, Holland, and were granted **asylum**. In 1620 a group of these Leyden Puritans led by William Brewster received a **land grant** from the Virginia Company, which allowed them to join others who were leaving for America. They agreed to be indentured servants to London investors for a number of years.

On September 16, 1620 the *Mayflower* set sail from England heading to Virginia. There were 102 men, women, and children on board. Fewer than half were Puritans, while the rest were adventurers or others who wished to leave England. Almost 180 years later, historians named these passengers Pilgrims.

Mayflower *approaching landfall.*

The male passengers sign the Mayflower Compact on board the ship in 1620 needing to establish a civil society.

A storm blew the ship northward, and on November 19 it landed near present-day Provincetown on Cape Cod. Believing themselves outside the domain of both the Virginia Company and the crown, they drafted a formal agreement called the Mayflower Compact. They agreed to abide by any just and equal laws their government might pass and to have the right to choose their own leaders.

They sailed a bit further, and on December 21 they landed at a spot that Captain John Smith had named Plymouth, on the coast of present-day Massachusetts. During the first winter they lost nearly half of their party to exposure and disease, but they decided to stay. The Wampanoag Native Americans were helpful and taught the settlers to grow maize, or corn. By the following year, the Pilgrims had a good crop of corn and had harvested furs and lumber to sell. Early leaders of this colony included John Carver, John Alden, and William Bradford, who was the colony's governor for more than 30 years.

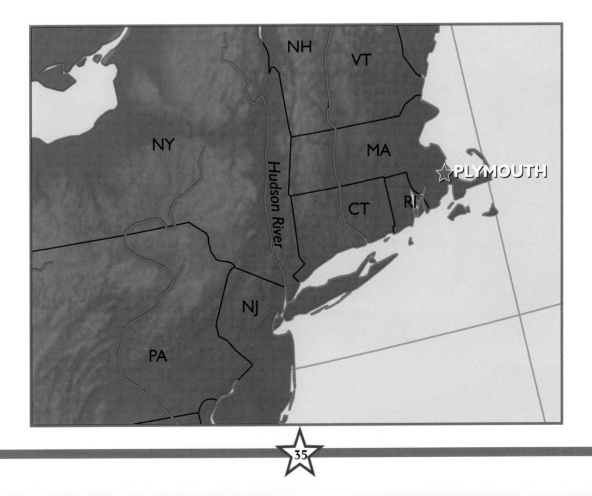

SQUANTO

The Pilgrims had planned to grow wheat in their new colony. But the crop would not grow in New England's rocky soil. A member of the Wampanoag named Tisquantum, or Squanto, taught them how to grow corn. He had traveled to England years before and learned English. Some months after the Pilgrims arrived, Squanto and his friend, Samoset, startled the newcomers by saying "Welcome" in English.

Squanto stayed with the Pilgrims for a few months, bringing them deer meat and beaver skins. He taught them about the local plants, how to dig clams and use fish for fertilizer, and hundreds of other survival skills.

Squanto helps a settler survive in an unknown land.

The colonies might not have grown had it not been for a great religious **emigration** from England in the 1630s. About one thousand immigrants, mostly Puritans, arrived in 15 ships in 1630. Led by John Winthrop, they had a grant from Charles I to establish the Massachusetts Bay Colony. It was first located at present-day Salem,

Plaque set in remembrance of the founding of the Massachusetts Bay Colony.

Massachusetts, and later moved to Boston. By the mid-1600s more than 15,000 Puritans had left England for America, seeking religious and economic opportunities.

The Puritans worked with merchants in England, who supplied them with credit to buy supplies. In return, they produced dried fish, cattle, and corn. When English support faded in 1637 because of political troubles, the settlers became more self-sufficient. They began a shipbuilding industry and sold products such as salted beef and dried fish to the West Indies, using the money to buy supplies in England. This trade sustained New England for many years. In 1684 the Massachusetts Bay Colony came under direct British rule and in 1691 merged with Plymouth and Maine, then a part of Massachusetts.

After the initial success of these settlements, other English colonies quickly formed. In 1632 Lord Baltimore founded Maryland, later called Baltimore, for Roman Catholics. In 1636 Roger Williams and Anne Hutchinson were expelled from Massachusetts for being too liberal. They and a few others founded Rhode Island. In 1639, New Haven, the future Connecticut, was formed.

By the mid-17th century, small groups of settlers were also living in the present states of New Hampshire and North Carolina. A South Carolina settlement founded in 1670 became Charles Towne in 1680 after King Charles II. This is now Charleston, South Carolina. By 1733, the 13 original colonies were in place, making up the core of what would become the United States of America.

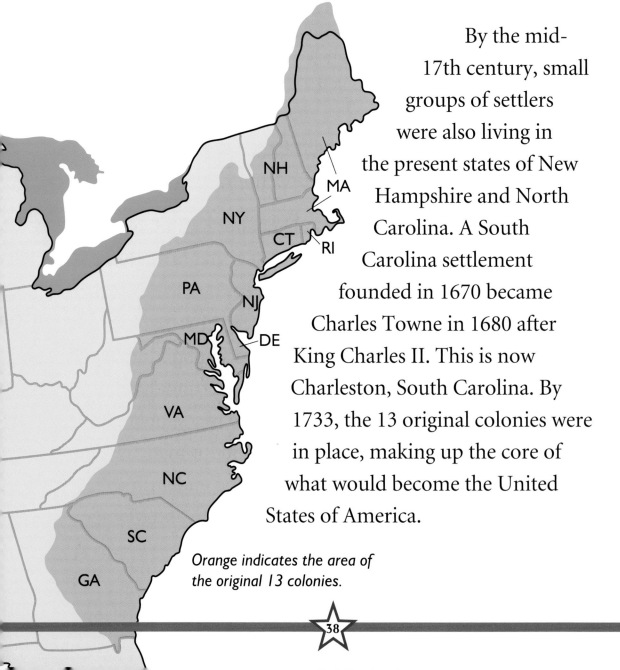

Orange indicates the area of the original 13 colonies.

Chapter 5
The Seeds of Democracy are Planted

In July of 1619 the first meeting of a representative government was held in America in Jamestown. To encourage the struggling colonists to stay, the Virginia Company permitted a certain degree of self-rule. The House of Burgesses was the result. The company appointed a governor, who then selected a council of six. Fifteen burgesses, representatives from different districts, made up the rest of the general assembly. At first they were landowners from the larger plantations. Only free men more than 17 years old could vote for the burgesses.

Patrick Henry Treason speech before the House of Burgesses.

The Massachusetts colony also took important steps toward democracy. It developed a statement of individual rights that became the basis for the Bill of Rights in the U.S. Constitution. The Plymouth Colony's General Fundamentals called for annual elections and specified that anyone accused of a crime must be tried by a **jury**. Also, no colonists would be taxed without being represented in the government. The Massachusetts Body of Liberties, adopted in 1641, also said that people should not have to **incriminate** themselves and that nobody would be deprived of life, liberty, or property except by due process of law.

These seeds of democracy may be due to England's promises to the colonists. The first charter of the Virginia Company in 1606 assured colonists and their descendants "all liberties… as if they had been abiding and born within this our realm of England." One such liberty was trial by jury and another was having some say over taxation. The colonists eventually expanded on these freedoms to create a more democratic form of government than any that existed in Europe at the time.

Those who sailed for America were often rugged individualists who expected to find themselves in an uncivilized wilderness without laws, institutions, or even support from their parent country. They were prepared to form their own government and laws. The Puritans brought with them an intense desire for religious freedom. Yet, most of the colonies did not practice it themselves. The idea of **tolerating** other systems of belief was **radical**. Of all New England's founders, only Roger Williams, Lord Baltimore, and William Penn publicly called for religious tolerance. Later in the 18th century, there were so many different churches that tolerance began to be more accepted.

The New World was a place where many different cultures competed and clashed with one another. Settlement attempts sometimes succeeded and often failed. As early settlers moved on and more European immigrants arrived, the country's growth advanced steadily in one direction, westward toward the setting sun.

FREE EDUCATION

Free education is one of New England's lasting contributions to the United States. By 1642, parents were required to teach their children to read and write. By 1647 every settlement with more than 50 families had to appoint a schoolmaster, who taught Latin and Greek grammar and literature as well as arithmetic. Four of these early schools, Boston Latin, Cambridge Latin, Roxbury Latin, and Hopkins Grammar School of New Haven, still exist today as high schools.

Biographies

Many people played important roles throughout this time period. Learn more about them in the Biographies section.

Cabot, John (1450-1498) - Italian-born navigator and explorer employed by Henry VII of England. His explorations gave England claims to America.

Menendez de Aviles, Pedro (1519-1574) - Spanish explorer who established the settlement of St. Augustine, Florida (1565). He became Florida's first Spanish governor.

Drake, Francis (1540-1596) - English sailor and adventurer who raided Spanish ships and colonies in the Caribbean.

Brewster, William (1567-1644) - Pilgrim religious leader, signer of the Mayflower Compact, and leader at Plymouth Colony.

Champlain, Samuel de (1567-1635) - French explorer, founder of New France and Quebec (1608).

Smith, John (1580-1631) - English soldier and colonial leader, first head of the Jamestown colony; explored the New England coast and gave the region its name.

Rolfe, John (1585-1622) - English colonist, the first to cultivate tobacco in Jamestown.

Bradford, William (1590-1657) - Colonial governor and signer of the Mayflower Compact. His *History of Plimoth Plantation, 1620-1646* is the basis for all accounts of the Plymouth Colony.

Samoset (1590-1653) - A Mohegan Native American who knew some English and greeted the Pilgrims by saying "Welcome."

Squanto (died 1622) - Pawtuxet Indian of Massachusetts, acted as interpreter for the Pilgrims of Plymouth Colony and helped them learn to survive.

Hutchinson, Anne (1591-1643) - English colonist and religious leader. Banned from the Massachusetts Bay Colony for her views, she helped settle Portsmouth, Rhode Island.

Pocahontas (1595-1617) - Daughter of Chief Powhatan and wife of Jamestown settler, John Rolfe.

La Salle, René-Robert Cavelier, Sieur de (1643-1687) - French explorer in North America. First to explore the Mississippi to its mouth, he claimed the land for Louis XIV of France (1682).

Penn, William (1644-1718) - Founder of Pennsylvania, became a Quaker in 1666 and was imprisoned several times for his religious views. Designer of the city of Philadelphia.

Timeline

1497
John Cabot sails along the eastern shores of Canada, giving England a claim to North America.

1524
France sends Giovanni da Verrazano to explore the coastline of present-day Canada, establishing a French claim to North America.

1585-1587
Sir Walter Raleigh tries to colonize Roanoke Island in Virginia.

1598
Jacques Cartier explores the St. Lawrence River to the future sites of Quebec and Montreal.

1608
French navigator Samuel de Champlain founds a trading post at Quebec.

1614
First Dutch settlement, Fort Nassau, near future Albany, New York.

1620
The *Mayflower* arrives at Plymouth in what is now Massachusetts.

1630
The first wave of thousands of new Puritan colonists arrive and the Massachusetts Bay Colony is established.

1733
All of the 13 original American colonies have taken shape.

1513
Spanish explorer Juan Ponce de León sights the North American continent and calls it La Florida.

1565
The oldest permanent European settlement in the United States is founded at St. Augustine, Florida.

1590
Rescuers find that all Roanoke colonists have vanished.

1607
The *Susan Constant*, *Godspeed*, and *Discovery* bring the first colonists to Jamestown.

1613
John Rolfe saves Jamestown by introducing a new strain of tobacco.

1619
The Dutch bring the first slave ship to the North American continent.

1626
First Dutch settlers on what is now Manhattan Island. Peter Minuit buys the island from Native Americans for trade goods worth 60 guilders (about $24 dollars).

1664
Stuyvesant surrenders New Netherland to England and it is renamed New York.

Reference

Imperial Exploration, 1400-1700

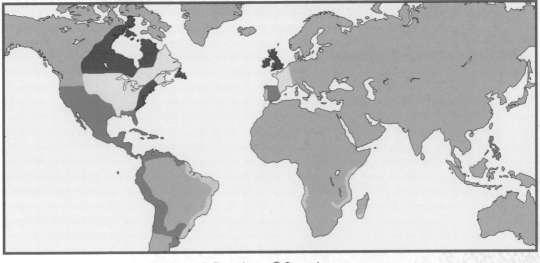

- ⚪ French
- ⚫ British
- ⚫ Spanish
- ⚪ Portuguese

Colonial Settlement in North America to 1750

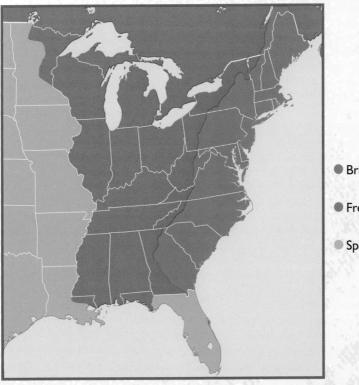

- ⚫ British Territory
- ⚫ French Territory
- ⚪ Spanish Territory

Websites to Visit

larryferlazzo.com/geography.html

www.cliffsnotes.com/more-subjects/history/us-history-i

www.humanjourney.us/america.html

Show What You Know

1. Who was Ponce de Leon?

2. When did the *Mayflower* arrive in Plymouth?

3. Who were the Puritans?

4. What did Squanto teach the Pilgrims?

5. Who brought the first slave ship to the North American continent?

Glossary

annex (AN-ex): to add territory by conquest or occupation

asylum (uh-SYE-luhm): a place of shelter and protection

charter (chahr-tuhr): a grant or guarantee from a state or country

convict (KAHN-vikt): a person who has been found guilty of a crime

emigration (im-uh-GRA-shuhn): the movement of a person or group away from a place or country

frigate (FRI-git): a light boat driven by sails; a small warship

horde (HORD): a crowd or swarm

in earnest (in er-nuhst): having a determined and serious state of mind; sincere

incriminate (in-krim-uh-NATE): to charge with a crime or show proof of involvement in a crime or fault

intermediary (in-tuhr-MEE-dee-ary): a go-between or agent

jury (juhr-ee): a body of persons sworn to give a verdict according to the evidence presented

land grant (land GRANT): a transfer of land by the government to another party

Parliament (pahr-lu-muhnt): the law-making body of government in England

radical (rad-uh-kuhl): tending to extremes, for example in politics, desiring to make extreme changes in existing views or institutions

Reformation (REH-for-may-shuhn): a major change in western Christianity that developed between the 14th and 17th centuries. It had to do with moving away from the Roman Catholic Church

West Indies (west IN-deez): name for the Caribbean Islands

Index